D0936173

POP CULTURE

American Life and Music from Elvis Presley to Lady Gaga

MARK MUSSARI

Cavendish
Square
New York

Published in 2014 by Cavendish Square Publishing, LLC
303 Park Avenue South, Suite 1247, New York, NY 10010

First Edition

Website: cavendishsq.com

This publication represents the opinions and views of the author based on his or her personal experience,
knowledge, and research. The information in this book serves as a general guide only. The author and
publisher have used their best efforts in preparing this book and disclaim liability rising directly or indirectly
from the use and application of this book.

CPSIA Compliance Information: Batch #WS13CSQ

All websites were available and accurate when this book was sent to press.

Library of Congress Cataloging-in-Publication Data

Mussari, Mark. • Popular music / Mark Mussari.
p. cm. — (Pop culture) • Includes bibliographical references and index.
Summary:"Provides a comprehensive look at the history of
popular music in America"— Provided by publisher.
ISBN 978-1-60870-922-9 (hardcover)—ISBN 978-1-62712-122-4 (paperback)—
ISBN 978-1-60870-927-4 (ebook)
1. Popular music—History and criticism. I. Title. II. Series.
ML3470.M899 2013 • 781.640973—dc23 • 2011020743

Series Consultant: Mark Mussari • Art Director: Anahid Hamparian
Series Designer: Alicia Mikles • Photo research by Lindsay Aveilhe

The photographs in this book are used by permission and through the courtesy of:
Cover photo by Michael Ochs Archives/Getty Images and Wong Maye-E/AP Photo;
Michael Ochs Archives/Corbis: p. 4; Photo by NBC Television/Getty Images: p. 8; Pictorial Press Ltd/
Alamy: p. 11; SHNS photo/courtesy MCA Records/Newscom: p. 12; Photos 12/ Alamy: p. 15;
Everett Collection: p. 16, 18; t14/ZUMA Press/Newscom: p. 21; Bettmann/Corbis: p. 23; Michael Ochs
Archives/Getty Images: p. 24; AP Photo: p. 26; Terry O'Neill/Hulton Archive/Getty Images: p. 27; Trinity
Mirror/Mirrorpix/Alamy: p. 29; AP Photo: p. 31; Howard Ruffner/Time & Life Pictures/Getty Images:
p. 34; Jim McCrary/Redferns/Getty Images: p. 37; Roger Bamber/Alamy: p. 39; Pictorial Press Ltd/Alamy:
p. 43; Denis O'Regan/ Getty Images: p. 45; Fin Costello/Redferns/Getty Images: p. 47; Eric Blum/Michael
Ochs Archives/Getty Images: p. 49; CBW/Alamy: p. 50; MSI Mirrorpix/Newscom: p. 53; Neal Preston/
Corbis: p. 54; Moviestore collection Ltd/Alamy: p. 55; Pictorial Press Ltd/Alamy: p. 57; Ebet Roberts/
Redferns/Getty Images: p. 61; Reed Saxon/AP Photo: p. 62; S.I.N./Alamy: p. 67; AF archive/Alamy: p. 69;
Steve Eichner/WireImage/Getty Images: p. 73; Reuters/Corbis: p. 76; AP Photo/Ben Margot: p. 78; KRT/
Newscom: p. 79; Evan Agostini/AP Photo: p. 83; Pictorial Press Ltd/Alamy: p. 84.

Printed in the United States of America

Contents

Introduction

Rock and roll is here to stay
It will never die
It was meant to be that way
Though I don't know why
I don't care what people say
Rock and roll is here to stay.
—Danny and the Juniors (1958)

MUSIC HAS ALWAYS PLAYED a powerful role in American culture, especially in the period following World War II (1939–1945). Since then, as consumer culture in the United States has grown, popular music—music with broad public appeal distributed mostly through record labels—has had a profound effect on people's lives and on the culture that surrounds them.

Starting in the 1950s—but with roots in earlier forms of music—rock and roll paved the way for the growing youth culture that would both determine music's direction and be influenced by music for decades to come. Although the early stages of rock and roll may seem innocent in retrospect, this new form of popular music initially appalled many Americans. Yet early rock and roll was only the tip of the iceberg.

Starting in the 1950s, the new sounds of rock and roll ushered in a post–World War II focus on youth culture. Dancing to the jukebox at the soda shop became a common custom.

In the decades that followed, from the turbulent 1960s to the materialistic 1980s to our current world dominated by social networking, popular music has been an important reflection of our changing culture and shifting values. In some instances, music has inspired some of those changes, leaving a record (in every sense of the word) of changing life in the United States in the second half of the twentieth and the early twenty-first centuries.

THE 1950s:
Youth Culture and the Birth of Rock

WHEN ELVIS PRESLEY FIRST SHOOK HIS HIPS on the *Ed Sullivan Show* in 1956, he ushered in America's preoccupation with popular culture in more ways than one. The television show reached a national audience, cutting across geographic boundaries. Presley was the first true national icon of rock and roll: a young, handsome performer with limitless energy whom young girls could dream of and young men could admire. But Presley's music actually came from other roots, and his powerful image was the beginning of a major shift in American culture.

POSTWAR UNITED STATES AND CONSUMERISM

Following World War II, the United States experienced a boom in population growth and in the economy. Soldiers who fought in the war returned home and slowly they began to find jobs. Demand for goods began to increase, as did marketing and advertising. As the economy grew, people started families—sometimes large ones—and many began to move out of cities and into the suburbs. Cars became an essential element of the American lifestyle. Highways were constructed, suburbs

grew, and schools were built to accommodate all these new children.

The first wave of the generation now called "baby boomers" had been born. In their children, the World War II generation of Americans had created a new, much larger group of consumers ready to buy clothes, toys, books, and music. By 1958 one-third of the U.S. population consisted of teenagers—and advertisers realized they could make more money by targeting teenagers rather than their parents. The growth of television and children's programming in the same decade gave advertisers the perfect outlet to reach this new, young audience.

ROCK-AND-ROLL SETUP

Before the 1950s, popular music was produced primarily for an adult audience. Singers including Frank Sinatra, Nat King Cole, and the Andrews Sisters sang standards and show tunes—often ballads or slow- and mid-tempo songs about romance featuring a lot of strings and dreamy arrangements. The Tin Pan Alley writers of the 1920s, '30s, and '40s—early composers of popular music—had written many songs for stage and screen musicals that also became successful on the radio. Sometimes these writers employed elements of other forms of music, such as classical or jazz.

Therefore, long before rock and roll appeared in the 1950s, a market existed for popular music, but it was not geared directly toward young people. All that would change after World War II.

Elvis Presley made what had been called "race music," or blues, jazz, and gospel sung and performed by African Americans, into a mainstream phenomenon. It didn't hurt that Presley had a voice so good, and a presence so magnetic, that even a real hound dog listened to him sing "Hound Dog" on *The Steve Allen Show* in 1956.

ROOTS I: RACE MUSIC AND RHYTHM AND BLUES

Blues and jazz music became increasingly popular after 1920. These styles of music were extremely rhythm-based and had their origins in African American culture.

In the South, gospel and spiritual music were given voice by African Americans, many of whom were the descendants of slaves. Blues music took its rhythms from African styles, with an emphasis on the backbeat (second and fourth beats in a four-beat musical measure). With songs about heartbreak, loneliness, and disappointment, the blues expressed universal feelings and concerns.

Jazz was a more sophisticated musical genre, rising out of clubs and bars in cities like Chicago and New Orleans. While jazz employs some elements of blues music, it relies more heavily on improvisation and skilled musicianship. The musicians who made jazz music popular—Louis Armstrong, Duke Ellington, Benny Goodman—became stars in their own time. Jazz lingo even entered American language as slang, an early example of music's effect on language. People who were cool were "hip to the jive" and nightclubs were called "joints."

In time, some musicians began to merge elements of jazz and blues, creating a new form of music: rhythm and blues. Much of this music, along with boogie-woogie, became known as "race music" because of its association with black musicians and its popularity in black communities.

ROOTS II: COUNTRY AND WESTERN

In the rural South, country music—with its origins in Celtic folk music and regional sounds—was a basic part of the culture. Many of the earliest rock-and-roll stars began as country performers, and that influence became a strong one in their music. In the 1950s, young Southern musicians started to merge traditional country sounds with rock rhythms. This

CALL-AND-RESPONSE

African American slaves working in the fields often sang in call-and-response—a style requiring a leader who sings a line and a group of singers responding with the same line or with an answer to the leader's question. Slaves later used this technique in the gospel music they sang in Christian churches. This same approach found a happy home in popular music, especially in rhythm and blues and the more commercial soul music. For example, a lead singer (like Smokey Robinson) would sing a line to a group of backup singers (like the Miracles) who then sang it back to him.

Smokey Robinson and the Miracles were a very popular singing group in the 1960s. They made famous a style called call-and-response that had originated with slaves working the fields in the South. In it, the leader sings a line and the others in the group either sing it back or answer it, sort of like a Greek chorus in theater.

music became known as "rockabilly" (a combination of "rock" and "hillbilly").

Elvis Presley brought rockabilly into the national consciousness with such hits as "Heartbreak Hotel" and "Hound Dog" (both in 1956). The influence of country music on popular music became even clearer as the 1950s progressed. Acts like Buddy Holly, the Everly Brothers, Brenda Lee, and Roy Orbison had backgrounds in country music, and their sounds were undeniably influenced by that experience. Yet rockabilly was also appreciated by young listeners from Maine to Michigan to Washington State, which gave them all a common interest, regardless of geography, socioeconomic status, race, or age. Popular music was helping to erase regional barriers.

In addition to gospel and soul, country music had a large influence on early rock and rollers, one of the most prominent of whom was Buddy Holly. He died tragically in a plane crash in 1959, along with both the Big Bopper and Ritchie Valens, who was best known for the song "Donna." The music of these musicians, however, lives on.

ELVIS AND HIS PELVIS

When Presley first appeared on the *Ed Sullivan Show*, one of the most successful variety shows in television history, the producers were so worried about his suggestive gyrations that they only allowed camera-men to shoot the young Mississippi-truck driver *from the waist up*! Today we would find his moves tame, to say the least. Bob Dylan once said that hearing Elvis for the first time was "like busting out of jail."

MARKETING MUSIC—BEYOND RACE

Wanting to enjoy the success of rhythm and blues music, some white artists singing popular music copied the styles of African American musicians, and in some cases re-recorded their songs to make them softer and more accessible to white audiences. Still, a number of early black artists became popular rock-and-roll icons, reaching national audiences and selling records to young people of all races. These artists include Chuck Berry, Little Richard, and Fats Domino, the early architects of rock and roll.

In hits like "Maybellene" (1955) and "Roll Over Beethoven" (1956), Chuck Berry gave the music world the very building blocks of rock and roll—including that all-important emphasis on the guitar.

TWO THREADS MERGE

In time, rhythm and blues and country music merged into rock and roll, which used characteristics of both forms of music. Rock and roll brought these regional styles together and turned them into a national phenomenon. Music played on transistor radios, portable turntables, and jukeboxes. It played on television, at dances, and in living rooms all across the United States and abroad (popular American music had far-reaching effects on other cultures). As one early rock song proclaimed, rock and roll was here to stay.

ROCK AROUND THE CLOCK

The relationship between rock and roll music and American culture became clearer as the 1950s progressed. A singer named Bill Haley recorded one of the earliest rock songs in 1951: "Rocket 88." But it was a song he recorded in 1954 with his group Bill Haley & His Comets—"Rock Around the Clock"—that would usher in much more than just a new genre of popular music.

"Rock Around the Clock" became a minor hit when it was featured in a 1955 movie, *Blackboard Jungle*, which was about juvenile delinquents defying the authority of their teachers. Growing up in the conservative environment of the 1950s, young audiences loved the film—but they especially loved "Rock Around the Clock," which was played loudly in the theater. By 1956 the song had sold an unbelievable 6 million copies, becoming the first certified national "hit" of the rock era.

Through this song, the growing population of American teenagers discovered a music that spoke both directly to them and to the rebellious nature of adolescence. Movies like *The Wild One* (1953) and *Rebel Without a Cause* (1955)—and even Broadway musicals like *West Side Story* (1957) with its gang-related plot—reinforced the image of the more dangerous side of youth.

AMERICAN BANDSTAND

In the 1950s television became a significant tool for distributing popular music through variety programs and dance shows. The most popular dance show for teens was *American Bandstand*, which began in Philadelphia in 1952. By the time Dick Clark became the host in 1957, *Bandstand* was telecast nation-

The theme song of the 1956 movie *Rock Around the Clock* became an anthem for the teens of the late 1950s.

ally, five days a week for ninety minutes in the late afternoon, exactly the time teenagers would be getting home from school.

Bandstand showcased the latest songs and musicians— and even more importantly, it featured a lot of dancing. Across the nation, *Bandstand* united teens in their love for all things rock and roll. Clark, who also produced the show, became a powerful figure in the music industry and one of the most recognizable Americans in the world. He hosted *American Bandstand* for more than thirty years: from 1957 until the show ended in 1989.

Kids and teens throughout the United States rushed home from school every day in the 1950s and 1960s to turn on, and sing and dance to, *American Bandstand*.

MONEY TO BURN

According to one statistic, teenagers in the 1950s were spending more than $9 billion a year. They received $6 billion from their home allowances and another $3 billion from their own earnings. Raised on early television toy commercials, teens of the 1950s became America's first mass consumers—an easy target for advertisers and merchants.

EARLY BACKLASH

Not everyone was happy about the growing popularity of rock music and its effect on American culture. A conservative backlash against this rowdy new music took shape as the 1950s advanced. FBI director J. Edgar Hoover called rock "a corrupting influence" on American youth. In 1956, the *New York Daily News* called rock "the music of delinquents" and criticized it for its "jungle-beat rhythms." The magazine *Music Journal* deemed rock a "menace to morals."

Segregationists—people who opposed the mixing of races—even called for a ban on rock and roll, perhaps recognizing that the music that had merged black rhythm and blues with white country music was bringing people together. Still, rock and roll *was* here to stay, and its cultural influence over the next five decades would be far-reaching.

The 1960s were a time of great change and turbulence. With the passage of the 1964 Civil Rights Act, African Americans gained significant rights. In this picture, singer Aretha Franklin and civil rights activist Martin Luther King Jr. pose together at a civil rights event.

THE 1960s:
Rock and Rebellion in a Decade of Change

MENTION THE 1960S AND MOST PEOPLE conjure up images of protests, wars, assassinations, and riots. While many of these events did shape the culture of the 1960s, the decade was much more diverse than one might think. In many ways, the decade's early years actually resembled the suburban innocence and prosperity of the 1950s.

Still, changes were brewing beneath the surface—changes that would have profound cultural effects on American life. Political and social unrest grew because of U.S. involvement in an ongoing civil war in Vietnam and desegregation laws enacted by the U.S. Supreme Court. Tensions eventually spilled onto the streets as protests and riots. Meanwhile, more women were entering the workforce and demanding equal rights, and African Americans were proudly proclaiming that "black is beautiful." The counterculture movement that would come to be known as the hippie movement grew as the 1960s progressed, and many different forms of popular music, especially folk and rock and roll, reflected the rapid changes occurring in society.

TEEN IDOLS

As the 1960s began, popular music seemed like an extension of the late 1950s. In 1960, the hottest dance craze was the Twist, introduced by Chubby Checker in his mammoth hit of the same name. The dance became a national sensation and continues to be one of the most recognizable dance movements in modern history.

As a response to the more raucous rock music of Jerry Lee Lewis and Little Richard, a crop of teen idols—young, attractive white singers whose singing style was similar to the crooners of the 1940s—began to top the music charts. These singers included Fabian, Frankie Avalon, Bobby Rydell, Paul Anka, and Ricky Nelson. Their mellow music became enormously popular, attracting legions of young female fans and compelling teenage boys to copy the singers' hairstyles and dress. Yet in retrospect, their innocuous popularity may have helped set up what was about to happen both musically and culturally.

CROSSING RACIAL BARRIERS: SWEET SOUL MUSIC

The civil rights movement struggled to bring equality to all Americans regardless of race. Congress passed the Civil Rights Act in 1964. Although teenagers of all races were wild for African American rockers like Chuck Berry and Little Richard, it took a former boxer/auto worker from Detroit to craft a musical sound that would truly break all barriers of race and age.

In 1958 Berry Gordy started Motown Records in a rented house that he called "Hitsville, U.S.A.," in Detroit, Michigan. Gordy wanted to bring rhythm and blues to black and white

It seemed that everyone in America was doing "The Twist," which was sung by Chubby Checker, played constantly on the radio, and danced to on *American Bandstand*.

listeners alike on a large-scale basis. To this end, he helped to create soul music, a sound merging rhythm and blues with elements of jazz, rock, and pop.

A one-time Ford employee, Gordy applied assembly-line production techniques to what became known as the Motown Sound. Motown was a shortening of "Motor Town," a nickname for Detroit, the automobile-producing capital of the world. Gordy had incredible resources to work with: an extraordinarily talented crop of young, aspiring, African American musicians from Detroit. Soon, Motown artists including Mary Wells, Marvin Gaye, the Supremes, Stevie Wonder, the Marvelettes, the Four Tops, Smokey Robinson and the Miracles, Martha & the Vandellas, and the Temptations began to dominate the record charts.

Add a house band of accomplished musicians and first-class songwriters like Smokey Robinson and the trio of Lamont Dozier and Eddie and Brian Holland, and Gordy (who also wrote some hit songs) had found the key to artistic and commercial success.

PREACHER'S DAUGHTER

Meanwhile at Atlantic Records, another budding record label for rhythm and blues artists, a young singer named Aretha Franklin—the daughter of a Detroit Baptist pastor—had recorded a number of hit records with a more determined soul sound. Her hit singles included "Chain of Fools" and "Respect" (both in 1967). In some ways, Franklin's career reflects the over-arching change in popular music in the 1960s. She had begun as a singer of traditional pop ballads at Columbia Records in the early 1960s, but success came when she used the full, raw power of her enormous, gospel-trained voice in her Atlantic releases.

MOTOWN REIGNS SUPREME

Diana Ross, Mary Wilson, and Florence Ballard—the three young women who were the Supremes—came from a housing project in Detroit. With their number one hit "Where Did Our Love Go" in 1964, they began their string of twelve number one singles—only the Beatles had more number ones that decade. More importantly, the trio sang at renowned supper clubs and other musical venues previously closed to black performers. Thanks to their exuberant stage presence and great talent, the Supremes created an indelible cultural image, particularly for black women—but also for any female singing group to follow in their glorious footsteps.

The Motown Sound became pervasive in the United States in the mid–1960s. The breakout group was the Supremes, three very appealing young African American women with great voices.

ON THE BEACH

Another musical slice of early 1960s Americana came from the West Coast with the Beach Boys, a band consisting of the three Wilson brothers (Brian, Carl, and Dennis), their cousin Mike Love, and Al Jardine. Their first hit "Surfin'" (1961) led to a string of songs about the beach, cars, and girls (until they took a different direction with *Pet Sounds* in 1966). Their early records featured catchy melodies written mostly by Brian Wilson, along with the band's tight and often complex vocal harmonies, a layered sound unique to them. The Beach Boys' success opened the door for other West Coast acts—such as Jan and Dean and the Ventures—moving rock out of the cities and onto the beach.

It seemed that every region of the United States developed its own distinctive rock sound. From California, the Beach Boys, three of whom were brothers, popularized the mellow sounds of the beach. Because of them, surfing became a major pastime of 1960s youth.

THE END OF INNOCENCE

With President John F. Kennedy in the White House and the American economy booming, the early 1960s were a time of great prosperity and growth. When President Kennedy was assassinated on November 22, 1963, the country was shaken by the tragic event. Many historians believe that the assassination and the events that followed laid the groundwork for a major cultural shift in the United States. The country as a whole had lost the wide-eyed innocence that developed during the 1950s and early 1960s, and popular music began to reflect this change.

THE BEATLES

A musical invasion hit America's shores in early 1964 when the Beatles (John Lennon, Paul McCartney, George Harrison, and Ringo Starr) first appeared on the *Ed Sullivan Show*. The four young men from Liverpool, England, had an effect far beyond Elvis's hip-shaking debut in the 1950s. More than 73 million Americans watched the Beatles on *Ed Sullivan*—almost half the country!

Having already experienced success in England, the Beatles introduced "mod"—a British style of music and dress—to the United States, and the country responded with wild enthusiasm. Known as "the Fab Four" and "the Mop Tops" (for their long boyish bangs), the Beatles became a worldwide cultural phenomenon. "Beatlemania" swept the country: American teenagers began to wear their hair and dress like the Beatles, and they collected dolls, posters, cards, and other memorabilia with the band's images on them. Two films starring the foursome—*A Hard Day's Night* (1964) and *Help!* (1965)—did even more to solidify their mass appeal. No band had ever had such a profound cultural effect.

BEATLES SOUNDS

The Beatles, with John Lennon and Paul McCartney writing most of their material, became known for their ever-changing sound. The band's early music was an amalgamation of American rhythm and blues and pop written to rock beats. They even covered some early Motown songs. As their sound developed throughout the 1960s, their music became more complex, moving from the exuberant "Can't Buy Me Love" (1964) to pensive songs like "Eleanor Rigby" (1966). After experimenting with drugs and studying Eastern philosophy, the Beatles began to create more experimental, psychedelic sounds. By the time they released their album *Sgt. Pepper's Lonely Hearts Club Band* in 1967, the group had crafted the first conceptual rock album.

The invasion of the British "Fab Four" truly revolutionized music— in America, and the world. From their haircuts to their increasingly complex rock lyrics, the Beatles changed the way people thought about popular musicians.

BRITISH INVASION

The Beatles opened the door for other British groups, such as the Dave Clark Five, Gerry and the Pacemakers, and Herman's Hermits, to achieve success on the American music charts. These upbeat pop sounds demanded a counterpoint that reflected lost innocence—and one arrived in the Rolling Stones. Often referred to as the Stones, this group's demeanor and edgy rock sound recalled the more dangerous aspects of the early 1950s rockers. In addition, the Stones' music was more blues-based, rougher, and less "pop" than the early Beatles' sound.

The Rolling Stones followed the Beatles' incredible success in the United States, and soon the whole world seemed divided on the question of which was the greatest band—a division that continues to this day.

Mick Jagger, the Rolling Stones' lead singer, swaggered and strutted on stage with seemingly boundless energy—and he still does! With their driving mega-hit "(I Can't Get No) Satisfaction" in 1965, the band secured its singular place in the history of popular music by expressing the darker side of popular culture. More than forty years later, the Rolling Stones are still performing their ingenious blend of blues and rock. Many historians and rock aficionados consider the Rolling Stones the greatest rock band in history.

THE VIETNAM WAR AND FOLK MUSIC

In 1965 President Lyndon B. Johnson sent U.S. combat troops to Southeast Asia and ordered bombings in North Vietnam. As U.S. involvement in the Vietnam War escalated, more young men were drafted and sent to fight. Protest music—growing out of folk music—became increasingly popular among young listeners.

Folk music has deep roots as an American art form. Especially in the twentieth century, folk music became the music of the working class, finding voice in such influential artists as Woody Guthrie and Lead Belly. In the 1960s a group of artists began to emerge out of the folk scene in New York City's hip Greenwich Village community, including Simon and Garfunkel, Bob Dylan, and Joan Baez. When respected folk-singing trio Peter, Paul and Mary performed Dylan's "Blowin' in the Wind" at the massive Civil Rights March on Washington, D.C. in 1963, they brought Dylan's music into the national spotlight.

That same year, silver-voiced Joan Baez—a songwriter, activist, and folk musician in her own right—introduced Dylan at the Newport Folk Festival. In Dylan, American popular music found its poet laureate. Although folk music was often at odds with more commercial-sounding pop, Dylan's songs, with their demanding melodies, imagery-laden lyrics, and socially charged messages, crept into the national consciousness.

A COUNTRY DIVIDED

By the mid–1960s the country was becoming increasingly divided over U.S. involvement in the Vietnam War. Students began to organize protests and sit-ins on college campuses and elsewhere—and some of these became violent. To the older generation, young people seemed to be unraveling and losing their value system: Many began to experiment with drugs, "dropping out" of society, leaving school, and moving to communes. Dylan and the other folk musicians gave these young people a musical voice in their growing dissatisfaction with society and politics.

Bob Dylan was the poet and sage of folk and protest music. The teenager came out of Middle America seemingly to give voice to an entire generation fed up with the status quo. Joan Baez, a brilliant songwriter in her own right, first popularized Dylan's music with her angelic voice.

BOB DYLAN— AMERICAN POET

Bob Dylan has gone through a number of sounds during his long, prolific career. Even in the 1960s he moved from a pure acoustic folk sound to the advent of folk rock and the use of electric guitars to country. He was even booed on stage at the Newport Folk Festival for "going electric" in 1965 when he performed his new song "Like a Rolling Stone" with a rock band and an electric guitar. Yet his vast songbook includes some of the most influential music in recorded history: the anthem "The Times They Are a-Changin'" (1964), "Mr. Tambourine Man" (1965), and "Just Like a Woman" (1966). In the beginning of the twenty-first century, Dylan was still recording new music, touring, and winning Grammy awards.

ALTERNATIVE SOUNDS

As many young people became more rebellious and anti-establishment, popular music began to reflect these alternative approaches. In the mid– and late 1960s psychedelic music— growing out of images from the drug culture and the use of the hallucinogenic drug LSD—became increasingly popular. Some of this music was referred to as acid rock (acid is another name for LSD). Much of it emerged from the music scene in San Francisco, a haven for alternative lifestyles that attracted musicians from all over the country.

Jefferson Airplane, with its seductive-voiced lead singer Grace Slick, was one of the first acid-rock acts to achieve national acclaim. They were followed by the Grateful Dead, the Doors (with their deep-voiced, nihilistic front man Jim Morrison), bluesy Janis Joplin, and guitar virtuoso Jimi Hendrix. Album covers and posters exhibited wild colors and titles like Jefferson Airplane's *Surrealistic Pillow*. Musically, the counterculture was in full swing—and it had found its audience.

WOODSTOCK

The power of popular music reached a peak at a three-day outdoor concert held in Upstate New York in August, 1969. Promoters had expected only 50,000 attendees, but Woodstock—as the Woodstock Arts and Crafts Festival came to be known—drew almost *half a million* people. They had come to hear such bands as Crosby, Stills, Nash & Young; Janis Joplin; the Grateful Dead; Jimi Hendrix; and the Who. Despite inadequate bathrooms, lack of food, and torrential rains, Woodstock was a huge success—three days of peace, love, and music that made history.

The Woodstock festival attracted so many people that it closed down the entire New York State Thruway during the weekend it was held. Despite the rain, mud, and dearth of food, the festival became a symbol of all that was good in the 1960s youth revolution.

Soul music also began to reflect the societal changes of the late 1960s. At Motown, the Temptations merged soul and psychedelic sounds in "Cloud Nine" (1968), a song about dropping out of the difficult life in the ghetto. In 1969, the funk-soul group Sly and the Family Stone recorded "Everyday People," a song about social tolerance insisting on "different strokes for different folks." That same year the trio known as the Impressions asked listeners to consider their "Choice of Colors."

END OF AN ERA

There is something symbolic in the Beatles announcing their breakup at the end of the 1960s. The four lads from Liverpool had gone through many changes during the 1960s—from youthful mop tops to experimental artists. In many ways their sound and their shifting public personas both reflected and influenced the radical cultural changes occurring during the tumultuous decade. Popular music—like life in the United States—would never be the same.

THREE

THE 1970s:
Decade of Indulgence—Rock as Big Business

AS THE 1960s CLOSED, 1970 BECAME A YEAR OF even greater cultural change. Americans celebrated the first Earth Day, and the U.S. Congress passed the Clean Air Act. Without the approval of Congress, President Nixon launched the U.S. invasion of Cambodia. The National Organization for Women (NOW) held a Women's Strike for Equality in New York City.

As the decade progressed, so did anti-war demonstrations and student resistance. U.S. involvement in the Vietnam War finally ended in 1973, but by 1974 President Nixon—who had been reelected in a landslide vote in 1972—faced impeachment because of his involvement in the Watergate break-ins at the Democratic National Headquarters during the 1972 campaign. All of these events shook the nation and found further expression in popular music.

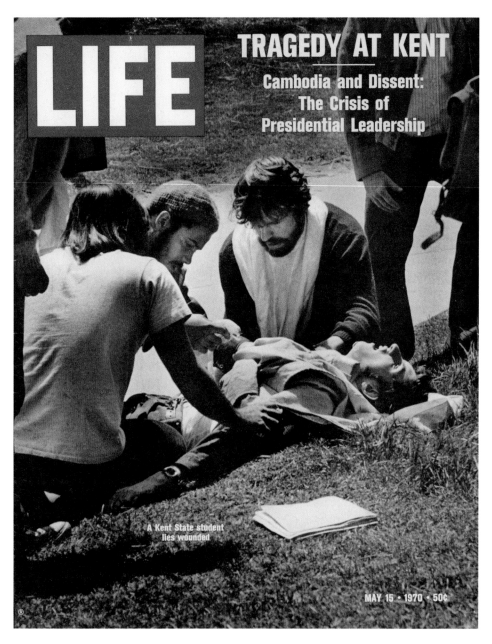

LIFE

TRAGEDY AT KENT

Cambodia and Dissent:
The Crisis of
Presidential Leadership

A Kent State student
lies wounded

MAY 15 • 1970 • 50¢

As the 1960s ended and the 1970s began, the mood of the nation grew darker. The death of four students during a protest against the Vietnam War sparked a deep anger toward the Establishment. That mood was immortalized in the Crosby, Stills, Nash & Young song "Ohio."

SOUNDS OF PROTEST

On May 4, 1970, the Ohio National Guard fired on student protestors at Kent State University, killing four students and injuring nine others. As a member of the folk-rock band Crosby, Stills, Nash & Young, Neil Young composed "Ohio," a protest song bemoaning the loss of the students' lives and holding President Richard Nixon responsible for the deaths. The song was originally banned on AM radio stations but found a home on the alternative FM stations that played progressive rock.

The following year Motown's Marvin Gaye, who had previously sung mostly love songs, released one of the most influential and inventive songs of the rock era: "What's Going On?" Employing twin-lead vocals, a jazzy sax line, and an atmospheric urban sound, Gaye produced an antiwar song that encapsulated the general feeling of the early 1970s and gave haunting voice to an existential uncertainty about the future.

THE BUSINESS OF ROCK

Rock music had been the voice of the counterculture movement in the 1960s. But Woodstock showed promoters and record executives that rock music could mean big business—rock bands could fill stadiums and sell millions of records. On the radio, programmers began to direct their shows toward specific target audiences for certain kinds of music. The record business was expanding, growing as much as 25 percent *a year* during the early 1970s.

SINGER-SONGWRITERS: BALLADEERS OF INTROSPECTION

In the 1960s many music acts recorded successful songs written by other people: songwriters Burt Bacharach and Jimmy Webb wrote huge hits for accomplished pop singers, including Dusty Springfield, Dionne Warwick, and the 5th Dimension. By the 1970s, some of this focus had changed to singer-songwriters—singers who wrote their own music and often played an instrument. Many of these artists had come from the folk tradition.

The 1970s has often been called "the Me Decade," a title referencing the self-absorption and narcissism that came to define the decade. Yet the introspection apparent in the music of some popular singer-songwriters also spoke to a more open attitude toward public expression of emotions. As the 1970s progressed and the first wave of baby boomers graduated from college, self-help books became increasingly popular; discussing feelings openly became a national pastime.

A TAPESTRY OF SONGWRITERS

One of the most successful albums in the early 1970s—and in all of recorded history—was Carole King's *Tapestry* (1971). Along with new songs she had written, King, a former songwriter of 1960s–pop hits, took some of her old songs and restaged them as ballads. The album spent an unbelievable 305 weeks on *Billboard* magazine's music charts and became a "must have" for college students across the United States—eventually selling more than 25 million copies.

Meanwhile, King's friend and longtime musical collaborator James Taylor crafted highly personal songs, often merging elements of folk, country, and rhythm and blues with imagery-laden lyrics and catchy melodies.

Carole King spent the early part of the 1960s writing songs that became hits for what were then known as "girl groups." In 1971 she branched out and became famous as the singer of her own tunes.

Writing about her personal experiences, Joni Mitchell took a confessional approach to folk rock. A painter, she crafted highly visual, poetic lyrics and later delved into experimental jazz sounds.

Laura Nyro was an influential singer-songwriter who emerged from the New York club scene in the late 1960s. She was most successful as a songwriter, and her songs were recorded with great success by a number of artists, including the 5th Dimension and Barbra Streisand.

The music of conservationist John Denver also reached a worldwide audience in the 1970s. Denver merged folk, pop, and country into an acoustic sound that had wide commercial appeal.

BOY WONDER GROWS UP

At Motown, the blind, multitalented musician Stevie Wonder took his career into his own hands and began to produce (or put the money up for) his own albums. Wonder was experimental on every front: he perfected the use of the synthesizer in popular music, and his lyrics addressed such topical issues as urban living, religious beliefs, and personal development. By the time he released his groundbreaking album *Innervisions* (1973), Wonder had grown into one of the most respected artists in the history of popular music.

EXPANSIONS: ELTON JOHN AND DAVID BOWIE

Two British singer-songwriters who expanded cultural boundaries in the 1970s were Elton John and David Bowie. With his broad theatricality, wild outfits, and energized stage presence, John—a classically trained pianist—was the perfect larger-than-life artist for the 1970s. Throughout the decade, he produced indelible hits, including "Your Song" (1970), "Tiny Dancer" (1971), "Daniel" (1973), and "Don't Let the Sun Go Down on Me" (1974). Over the next four decades, John would sell 250 million records, making him one of popular music's most successful artists.

As sexual mores changed in the latter 1960s and early 1970s, recording artists also began to test social boundaries. In glam rock, which developed in Britain during the early 1970s, both male and female performers wore makeup, outlandish outfits in satin or glitter, and huge platform shoes. In 1972 David Bowie began to record and perform as an alter ego— Ziggy Stardust, an androgynous persona he created for the glam-rock era. Although Bowie abandoned his Ziggy persona by the mid–1970s, he went on to become one of rock's most innovative artists.

David Bowie's gender-bending persona both foreshadowed and highlighted a change in the sexual mores and gender definitions beginning to become public in the 1970s.

POP CONFECTIONS

In addition to rock and folk sounds, popular music with broad commercial appeal also made headway in the 1970s. The brother-and-sister duo the Carpenters recorded contemporary pop music featuring strong melodies, layered harmonies, and Karen Carpenter's silky voice, a deeply emotive alto. The Carpenters sold millions of records throughout the 1970s, and many of their hits were used as prom themes and wedding songs across the United States.

Other acts achieved success with a mellow "adult" pop, including Barry Manilow, Canadian crooner Anne Murray, whose rich voice enabled her to cross over easily into the country music charts, and Australian singer Helen Reddy. Reddy's "I Am Woman" (1972) became an international anthem for the women's movement.

ABBA

Pop music's most successful act in the 1970s was the Swedish quartet ABBA, consisting of Benny Andersson, Agnetha Fältskog, Anni-Frid Lyngstad, and Björn Ulvaeus. Kicking off their careers by winning the Eurovision Song Contest in 1974, ABBA experienced unparalleled worldwide success throughout the decade, eventually selling more than 360 million records. Their song "Dancing Queen" (1976) topped the record charts in the United States, the United Kingdom, and eight other countries.

STADIUM ROCK: HEAVY METAL TAKES THE STAGE

The excess and self-indulgence of the 1970s also spilled over into rock music. Bands began to play large arenas—often stadiums intended for sporting events—and these venues demanded a huge sound to reach the thousands of fans in the audience. British bands Yes, Jethro Tull, Queen, Genesis, and Pink Floyd took an artsy, theatrical approach to rock and garnered tremendous followings for their musicianship and stage presence.

Meanwhile, heavy metal—a genre of rock characterized by loud guitars, pounding drums, distortion, and massive vocals—reached a pinnacle with Led Zeppelin, a band whose ornate song "Stairway to Heaven" (1971) became an anthem for lovers of stadium rock. Heavy metal and British rock bands alike tested the boundaries of rock music in both form and approach. Queen, Pink Floyd, and Genesis are among the best-selling artists in recording history.

In the United States, hard rock found its voice in Aerosmith, a Boston-based band fronted by Steven Tyler, who has experienced enormous success in a career spanning more than forty years. And KISS—with their cartoon-like makeup and wild stage shows—took theatricality to new heights.

REGIONAL SOUNDS

In the South, in Philadelphia, and in California, regional sounds began to make their mark on popular music, yet this regional music had wide appeal across the United States and abroad. Southern rock included the Allman Brothers, who merged elements of country and blues into a unique sound that would influence both rock and country music for decades to come. The hard-rocking Lynyrd Skynyrd also came out of the Southern rock genre. Skynyrd left the world two southern rock classics: "Freebird" (1973) and "Sweet Home Alabama" (1974).

In the mid–1970s a new urban soul sound emerged from Philadelphia, thanks to songwriters Thom Bell, Linda Creed, and the writing-producing team of Kenneth Gamble and Leon Huff. In 1972 the singing trio known as the O'Jays recorded "Love Train," a soul song pleading for an end to world conflicts.

In California, two of popular music's most successful acts actually grew out of one. In the early 1970s, Mexican American singer Linda Ronstadt enjoyed modest success with a group of musicians who would eventually become the Eagles. In time, Ronstadt went solo and became the most successful female artist of the 1970s and the first artist in history to have an album (*Living in the USA*, 1978) ship double platinum (2 million copies).

Meanwhile the Eagles, with their sharp studio musicianship and intricate harmonies, became one of the most successful acts in the history of contemporary music. Their song "Desperado" (1973), which Ronstadt also recorded, is considered a classic rock ballad. Over the next three decades, the band's *Their Greatest Hits (1971–1975)* album would go on to sell 29 million copies in the United States alone, making it one of the most popular albums in music history.

FLEETWOOD MAC

One of the most successful acts in the 1970s, Fleetwood Mac was originally a blues-based English band; then, founders Mick Fleetwood and John McVie, along with Christine McVie, added Americans Stevie Nicks and Lindsey Buckingham. The revitalized Fleetwood Mac produced bluesy pop sounds, gothic ballads, and driving rock songs. The band's stage presence—as well as Nicks's ethereal style—helped make them an international super group. Their album *Rumours* (1977) has sold an astonishing 40 million copies worldwide.

DISCO—LOVE TO HEAR PERCUSSION

When people call the 1970s "the Me Decade," they often think of disco music as a symbol for the excesses of that decade. Recreational drug use and sexual experimentation became increasingly popular among young people, and dance clubs seemed to speak directly to this culture, promoting nightlife and dancing.

The rhythms of disco actually grew out of 1960s dance music, which is heavily dependent on bass rhythms, and the urban nightclub scene (especially gay and African American clubs). In the 1970s artists merged Latin rhythms with heavy

SATURDAY NIGHT FEVER

The film *Saturday Night Fever*—about a young man in New York and his nightlife in the disco bar scene—was released in 1977. The film, starring John Travolta, was an instant success, as was its star-studded soundtrack. The Bee Gees, who had rock and pop hits in the 1960s, supplied much of the movie's music, including the hit "Stayin' Alive" and the ballad "How Deep Is Your Love." Eventually selling more than 15 million copies, the movie's soundtrack became one of the most popular ever released.

No music defined the 1970s as disco did, and nothing brought disco into the limelight like the movie *Saturday Night Fever*. Featuring music by the Bee Gees and dancing by John Travolta, it influenced an entire generation in terms of speech, fashion, and maybe even aspirations. Not to mention music.

orchestration into longer songs for the dance floor. Lyrics became less important, and an entire style of dress accompanied what came to be known as disco (a shortening of "discotheque," as dance clubs are called in Europe).

Artists of the 1970s who carved careers for themselves by producing songs that were hits both in dance clubs and on popular charts included Donna Summer, KC and the Sunshine Band, the Bee Gees, Gloria Gaynor, and Chic.

DISCO BACKLASH

Many hard-core rock fans were resistant to the slick music and glitzy styles of disco, and a backlash against the music occurred during the 1970s. Some radio DJs even called for the burning of disco records in the name of "real" rock and roll. Meanwhile, a more rebellious rock movement was slowly emerging in New York and London, and it would shift focus away from disco— although dance music in one form or another has never really lost its popularity.

PUNK ROCK

In many ways, punk rock seems almost inevitable in the face of the growing commercialism of rock and roll in the 1970s. Faced with weak economies in the United States and England, a number of young musicians began making angry, often cacophonous rock. This punk style was also reflected in their caustic attitudes and extreme dress. In the United States, New York City—particularly the bar CBGB in Manhattan's Lower East Side—became a center for punk rock in the mid–1970s. In time, acts such as the Clash, the Ramones, and poet and songwriter Patti Smith brought punk to a wider audience. In *The History of Rock and Roll*, Stuart A. Kallen describes the Ramones' music as "two-chord power pop sounding like psycho surfer music played by a demented Buddy Holly."

The antithesis of disco, punk rock—epitomized by groups such as the Ramones—emphasized an alienation from Establishment values that had first been voiced by folk musicians in the 1960s.

Punk reached its zenith with the British band the Sex Pistols and their notorious front men Johnny Rotten and Sid Vicious. The group's music was often obscene, anarchistic, and belligerent. Despite their short career and bad press following their breakup (Vicious was accused of murdering his girlfriend Nancy Spungen, and he eventually died from a heroin overdose), their music continues to have a strong cult following.

The Buggles' "Video Killed the Radio Star" was the first music video ever aired on MTV.

FOUR

THE 1980s:

Material Culture

BREAK DANCING. BIG HAIR. YUPPIES. PAC-MAN. MTV. Popular culture truly became a national pastime in the 1980s as technology brought rapid societal changes. Music remained at the forefront of these cultural changes, thanks in great part to the arrival of the music video on television. Although musicians had relied primarily on radio play, concerts, and record sales for success, videos altered the way consumers approached music. The medium was also a broader way to disseminate style—both musically and visually.

In videos the image moved to the center of music's attraction. Where many artists and record companies rose to the challenge of creating videos, some musicians saw this development as the end of music for music's sake. A video is, first and foremost, a commercial funded by a record company to sell music. Yet it is also an art form in its own right. Ironically, the first video played on MTV in 1981 was the prophetically titled "Video Killed the Radio Star" by the Buggles.

DECADE OF CHANGE

When Ronald Reagan was elected president in 1980, the economy was struggling, Americans were being held hostage in Iran, and baby boomers were now professionals with careers and families. Reagan's positive campaign messages resonated with voters both old and young, and ushered in a "feel-good" era for the nation.

In many ways, the 1980s was a decade of extremes. Upward mobility and the rise of materialism became driving forces in the decade—so much so that *Newsweek* magazine dubbed 1984 "the year of the Yuppie" (a shortening of "young, upwardly-mobile professional"). On the other hand, during the decade, musicians held massive concerts—like Live Aid in 1985—to raise funds for famine victims in Africa. The stock market crashed in 1987 and the AIDS epidemic became a horrifying reality all over the world.

MTV

It is almost impossible to overestimate the effect of videos on popular music during the 1980s. When the new cable station Music Television (MTV) premiered in August 1981, music lovers suddenly found their favorite artists and songs available on television. MTV forced established artists to step up their game visually. And perhaps more importantly, the network created a venue for new artists who were more video friendly. The venue also reflected popular music's movement toward technological or electric sounds.

In the early 1980s artists like Devo—an avant-garde quintet from Ohio—used aspects of performance art to create inventive videos with often unnerving images. The British band Culture Club, with its flamboyant lead singer Boy George, seemed perfectly suited to the visual form: their music blended elements of reggae and soul, and the gender-bending George loved the cam-

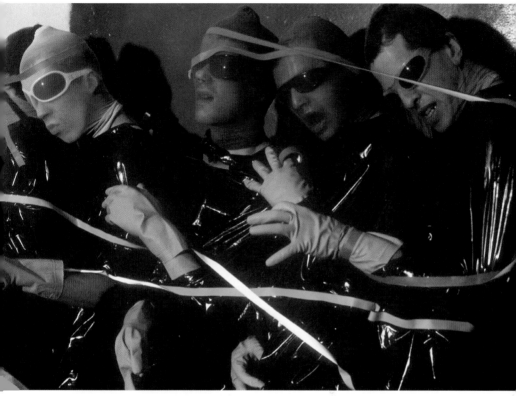

The early 1980s are synonymous with the rise of the music video. Groups such as Devo combined music with aspects of performance art, which was just hitting its stride.

era. Prior to video, Cyndi Lauper might have had to rely solely on her larger-than-life voice to achieve fame. But music videos enabled Lauper to create a colorful, almost cartoonish persona perfectly suited to the new, burgeoning medium.

NEW WAVE

In time, the punk rock of the late 1970s yielded to a more popular and less angry form of music known as new wave. The website allmusic.com defines new wave as pop music that was not part of the mainstream yet was "melodic, catchy, idiosyncratic, and quirky." These traits made new wave more accessible to the general public than the edgier punk. The video craze of the early 1980s also helped new wave bands reach a wider audience.

Perhaps the most popular band to emerge from the early new wave movement was Blondie, led by its smoldering lead singer and songwriter Debbie Harry. Their music represents a softening of punk styles into a more melodic sound that also involved synthesizers. New wave also found artistic expression in the innovative music and videos of the Talking Heads, who experimented with unusual electronic effects and African rhythms—as in their 1983 hit "Burning Down the House."

Other significant acts emerging from the new wave movement include the Cars, the Clash, and British singer-songwriter Elvis Costello. With his bespectacled geek-chic appearance, Costello resembled a new-wave version of the late Buddy Holly.

Debbie Harry and her band, Blondie, rode the top of the music known as new wave.

THEY HAD THE BEAT

One of the few all-girl rock groups to achieve worldwide fame also came out of the new wave movement: the Go-Go's. With their simple lyrics and driving beats, the band's hugely successful singles— "We Got the Beat" and "Our Lips Are Sealed" (both in 1981)—seemed like a throwback to the playful records of early rock and roll. The group also helped launch lead singer Belinda Carlisle's successful solo career. Carlisle had hits in the mid– and late 1980s.

SECOND BRITISH INVASION

In the 1980s the rise of new wave—coupled with the growing popularity of music videos—opened the door for a number of British bands to achieve worldwide success. Not since the Beatles and the British Invasion of the 1960s had so many British bands topped the American music charts. These bands included Duran Duran, Culture Club, ABC, Flock of Seagulls, the Cure, the Fixx, Bananarama, Spandau Ballet, and the Eurythmics (featuring lead singer Annie Lennox).

THE PRETENDERS

One of the most respected music acts of the 1980s was the Pretenders, formed in England and led by American-born singer-songwriter Chrissie Hynde. Hynde's punk-influenced makeup and clothes, along with her low alto voice and brooding delivery, drew millions of fans. Illustrating how rock music continued to enter mainstream culture, the Pretenders' song "Back on the Chain Gang" (1982) was used in the soundtrack to the film The King of Comedy (1983).

THE POLICE

The Police was another British band that came from the punk scene and then transcended it. They did so by mixing pop sensibilities with reggae and African rhythms. The trio crafted catchy tunes like "Don't Stand So Close to Me" and "Every Little Thing She Does Is Magic" (both 1981), but it was their lead singer, Sting, and his expressive voice that made them an international phenomenon. On their hugely successful album *Synchronicity* (1983), the trio created atmospheric, haunting numbers such as "Every Breath You Take" and "Wrapped Around Your Finger," securing the band's place in music history and launching Sting's solo career.

BLUE COLLAR TROUBADOURS: MUSICAL BACKLASH

In the 1980s, materialism came to define the United States, but nevertheless, a number of musicians remained highly critical of the Reagan administration and what they viewed as the politics of greed. The music of Bruce Springsteen, John Cougar Mellencamp, and Billy Joel reflects a populist approach similar to that of the 1960s folk singers. These three artists had their professional beginnings in the 1970s, but broad success came to them in the 1980s, when they gave musical voice to the plight of common men and women.

Springsteen, who hailed from a working-class background in New Jersey, had a major hit with "Born to Run" in 1975. His 1980 album *The River* finally brought him to the top of the record charts with his Dylan-influenced folk rock. In 1984 Springsteen's "Born in the U.S.A." became a national anthem for working-class people. The song was so popular that President Reagan asked to use it in his 1984 bid for reelection, but Springsteen refused.

FROM IRELAND—WITH LOVE

Ireland spawned one of rock's most enduring super-groups in the 1980s: the Dublin-based band U2. At a time when synthesized pop music was prevailing, U2 blended the political fervor of late–1960s rock bands with a complex and atmospheric approach to their music. Platinum-selling albums and successful singles led U2 to the Grammy Award in 1987 for Album of the Year for *The Joshua Tree*. Bono, the band's outspoken lead singer, has earned international respect as an activist for a number of causes, including peace, hunger, and alleviating third-world debt.

One of the supergroups of the 1980s, U2, pictured above in 1983, may now be most notable for spawning Bono (*second from right*), who has become famous over the decades for his charitable causes, and for, along with the Edge (*right*), being one of the creators of Broadway's *Spider-Man: Turn Off The Dark*.

Bruce Springsteen was an heir to both Bob Dylan's mantle and that of hard-driving rock groups like the Rolling Stones. Here he talks to a group of Vietnam vets, a group in whom the socially conscious rock star took a great interest.

Mellencamp came from a blue-collar background in Indiana and wrote angry, often biting protest songs about the plight of the disaffected worker. In songs such as "Pink Houses" (1983) and "Small Town" (1985), he addressed the shattered American dream and those lost within it in small-town USA.

In 1982 Billy Joel—known as the "Piano Man" for his musicianship and a 1973 song of the same name—produced the album *The Nylon Curtain*. It contained two socially conscious songs: "Allentown," about unemployed steelworkers in Pennsylvania, and "Goodnight Saigon," about the poor treatment of Vietnam War veterans, many of whom had become homeless by the 1980s. Springsteen's, Mellencamp's, and Joel's songs offer a critical counterpoint to the increasingly synthesized popular music of the 1980s.

KING OF POP: MICHAEL JACKSON

When Michael Jackson died suddenly at the age of fifty in 2009, he left behind one of the greatest legacies in popular music history. Along with four of his brothers, Jackson began his astounding career at the age of eleven as lead singer for the Jackson 5—the last successful Motown singing group to come out of the 1960s and 1970s. Early on, Jackson's limitless energy, loud voice, and astonishing dance skills indicated that he was a born entertainer. His commanding stage presence as well as broad showmanship showed influences of great rhythm and blues performers of the 1960s such as Jackie Wilson and James Brown.

In the 1970s Jackson began to record as a solo artist, producing a number of successful dance hits for the disco era. It was in the 1980s, however, that he became a pop artist to be

Michael Jackson's album *Thriller*, released in 1982, quickly became the best-selling album of all time.

reckoned with—particularly with the album *Thriller* (1982). By 1985, the *Guinness Book of World Records* had declared *Thriller* the best-selling album of all time. As of 2011 it has sold more than 100 million copies.

In his songs "Billie Jean" and "Beat It" (both from *Thriller*), Jackson's music began to become its own genre. His music was a hybrid of soul, rock, pop, techno, and dance, and his production techniques revealed an inventive, layered approach to popular music.

In addition, Jackson revolutionized the music video. Before him, very few black artists had been given airplay on MTV—but there was no denying the powerful visual effects and intricate dancing that defined Jackson's videos. As the 1980s progressed, Jackson became an international phenomenon unlike any seen since the Beatles, and he was soon crowned the "King of Pop."

"WE ARE THE WORLD"

In 1985 Michael Jackson and Lionel Ritchie cowrote what would become the best-selling single in music history to that date. "We Are the World" was written to raise money for the USA for Africa relief fund. Jackson and Ritchie gathered a star-studded group of artists—including Bruce Springsteen, Stevie Wonder, Tina Turner, Bob Dylan, and Diana Ross—to record the song and a video. "We Are the World" raised more than $50 million in 1985.

MATERIAL GIRL

Madonna—her very name conjures up shifting images of the pop icon—was born Madonna Ciccone in Bay City, Michigan.

In 1978 Madonna arrived in New York City with only $35 in her pocket and a firm belief in her own destiny. Trained as a dancer, she first pursued a career in that field but was soon writing her own music and making connections in New York's dance clubs. DJs in those clubs were the first to play Madonna's catchy, danceable music.

After her first hit, "Borderline" (1984), Madonna produced hit after hit of finely crafted pop songs that—combined with her strong visual appeal—proved a winning combination in the video age. Her cultural effect was far-reaching: young girls all over the world began to dress in Madonna's sexy vintage

Riffing on images of 1950s bombshells like Marilyn Monroe, Madonna rapidly became not just the "material girl" of the 1980s, but an icon of transformation for an entire generation.

style. Today her songbook includes some of the most recognizable pop tunes in the world: "Like a Virgin" (1984), "Material Girl" (1985), "Into the Groove" (1985), "Papa Don't Preach" (1986), and "Like a Prayer" (1989).

Throughout the 1980s Madonna reinvented her image, transforming herself from dance-club phenomenon to world-renowned actress and record producer. An international phenomenon and one of the highest-paid women in entertainment history, she frequently makes headlines by testing the limits of social boundaries.

AN ARTIST NAMED PRINCE

Another artist who pushed the cultural envelope in the 1980s was Prince—born Prince Rogers Nelson—a multitalented singer, musician, and composer from Minneapolis. Like Michael Jackson, Prince was as much a performer as he was a musician, evident in his boundless on-stage energy. Prince's sound was funk-based, owing to 1970s influences such as Parliament and Sly and the Family Stone.

In songs like "Little Red Corvette" and "1999" (both 1982), Prince merged new wave and soul by employing sexually playful lyrics and synthesized sounds. Prince wrote, acted in, and produced the film *Purple Rain*, released in 1984. The soundtrack spawned the number one hit "When Doves Cry," and the album became a huge success, winning multiple Grammy Awards and an Oscar for Best Original Song Score.

WOMEN ASCENDING

In addition to Madonna, a number of other women made notable contributions to pop music in the 1980s. Like Cyndi Lauper and Chrissie Hynde, Pat Benatar used her powerful voice to break through the glass ceiling for women in rock. A lead singer in Fleetwood Mac, Stevie Nicks crafted some highly successful, artsy solo albums throughout the decade. And Janet Jackson—Michael's sister—came into her own with her melodic and danceable tunes, including 1989's "Miss You Much."

Once considered a rock singer, Linda Ronstadt proved her versatility by recording three albums of traditional pop standards with conductor Nelson Riddle, who had worked with Ella Fitzgerald and Frank Sinatra. During the 1980s Ronstadt also recorded a traditional country album, *Trio*, with superstars Dolly Parton and Emmylou Harris. She also recorded a selection of Mexican folk songs in honor of her Hispanic heritage.

Following in the footsteps of her famous relatives Dionne Warwick and Aretha Franklin, Whitney Houston burst onto the scene in 1985 with her melodramatic voice and glamour. Her self-titled debut album was the best-selling ever by a new artist. Her hit songs, a blend of theatrical ballads ("Didn't We Almost Have It All") and danceable pop ("I Want To Dance with Somebody Who Loves Me"), made her one of the most successful acts of the decade.

DYNAMIC DUO

The duo Hall & Oates began performing in the 1970s—but their fame reached unprecedented heights in the 1980s. With songs like "You Make My Dreams Come True" (1981), "I Can't Go for That (No Can Do)" (1981), "Maneater" (1982), and "One on One" (1983), the two friends from Philadelphia—Daryl Hall and John Oates—became the most successful duo in popular music to date. Because they were white but sang a hybrid of soul, rock, and pop, critics called their music "blue-eyed-soul." Duos have a long history in rock and roll, beginning with the influential Everly Brothers in the 1950s. In the 1960s, acts like the Righteous Brothers and Sonny and Cher dominated the pop scene, as did the Carpenters and Captain & Tennille in the 1970s.

RAP: CONCRETE POETRY

Although rap is now a popular music genre among people of all ages and races, it originated in urban African American neighborhoods—especially in New York City's South Bronx. In her book *Black Noise: Rap Music and Black Culture in Contemporary America*, Tricia Rose describes rap music as "a black cultural expression that prioritizes black voices from the margins of urban America."

When it began in the late 1970s, rap belonged to the cultural phenomenon known as hip-hop, a youth culture that also involved graffiti and break dancing. Today the terms rap and hip-hop are often used interchangeably. Both terms refer to the skill of speaking lyrics in time to a pronounced beat, which may be synthesized or instrumental. This practice is known among hip-hop artists as emceeing.

DJ KOOL HERC

Hip-hop's founder was DJ Kool Herc, whose real name is Clive Campbell. Born in Jamaica but living in the Bronx, he invented hip-hop (or rap) in the early 1970s while playing records at his sister's birthday party. As a DJ, Herc liked to isolate the rhythmic "breaks" in a song—that section in which the lyrics stop and the beat takes over. He would play that section repeatedly, often switching between two copies of the same record on separate turntables. The style of reciting lyrics over this emphasized beat became known as rapping.

The poetry of rap first came to mainstream attention in the song "The Message," produced in 1982 by DJ and composer Grandmaster Flash with his group the Furious Five. The song's lyrics candidly expressed the alienation many people living in the black ghetto felt. Other influential rappers from the 1980s include Queen Latifah, Salt-N-Pepa, Tone-Loc, LL Cool J, Run-D.M.C, Beastie Boys, and Ice-T.

In 1988 MTV—which had been criticized for ignoring videos by black artists—began airing *Yo! MTV Raps* (which ran until 1995). The hip-hop trio Run-D.M.C. hosted the first episode, an instant hit with fans worldwide. By the end of the 1980s rap singles like Young MC's "Bust a Move" (1989) were reaching an audience far beyond the local urban scenes that had given birth to the hip-hop movement.

In the next decade, hip-hop would become a dominant force in popular music, and some of its stars—including LL Cool J, Will Smith, Ice-T, Snoop Dogg, and Queen Latifah—would become successful television and film stars.

The hip-hop group Run-D.M.C. hosted the first episode of the super-popular *Yo! MTV Raps*.

The 1950s merged with the 1990s when presidential candidate Bill Clinton picked up a saxophone and played an impressive version of Elvis Presley's "Heartbreak Hotel" on *The Arsenio Hall Show* in 1992.

THE 1990s:

Alternative Sounds, Divas, and Country-Pop

IN 1992 PRESIDENTIAL CANDIDATE Bill Clinton picked up a saxophone and played with the band on a late-night talk show hosted by comedian Arsenio Hall. Not only did the performance help to solidify the support of Clinton's youthful voting base, it also illustrated that the generation that grew up listening to rock and pop had come into adulthood. Clinton, at the age of forty-five, and his vice-presidential candidate Al Gore (age forty-four) would go on to win the White House that November.

As his campaign song Clinton had chosen Fleetwood Mac's driving "Don't Stop" from the album *Rumours* (1977). Fleetwood Mac performed at his inauguration, along with pop stars Michael Jackson and Aretha Franklin. Bob Dylan performed "Chimes of Freedom" on the steps of the Lincoln Memorial.

By the start of the decade, a war had begun to brew in the Middle East as a result of Iraq's 1990 invasion of Kuwait. The AIDS epidemic was, sadly, in full swing and spreading beyond the gay community, especially among women and in the African American community. In 1990 President George H. W. Bush signed the Americans with Disabilities Act into law, extending civil rights to the disabled. In 1993 Janet Reno became the first woman named U.S. Attorney General. In 1994 the first sexual abuse case was brought against Michael Jackson: though eventually settled out of court, the case drew Jackson into an ongoing nightmare of negative publicity.

AIDS—A FILM AND A SONG

In 1993 Hollywood released the first mainstream film dealing directly with AIDS: *Philadelphia*, starring Tom Hanks and Denzel Washington. Bruce Springsteen wrote and recorded the dark ballad "Streets of Philadelphia" for the film. That year Springsteen won both the Academy Award and the Golden Globe for Best Original Song, as well as Grammy awards for Song of the Year and Best Song Written for a Motion Picture.

Throughout the 1990s, popular music took a number of turns—both forward and backward. Boy bands consisting mostly of teenage and twenty-something singers found enormous success during the 1990s, whereas grunge—a rough, stripped-down approach to rock—offered an edgier counterpoint. Two country singers, Garth Brooks and Shania Twain, experienced unprecedented success in the commercial pop market, drawing millions of fans to the genre with their stadium-friendly take on country music. Rap music grew in popularity and even became contentious as loyalties to West and East Coast rap brought fatal consequences—particularly in the form of violent gangsta rap. The bubblegum pop sound of the early 1960s also made a comeback at the end of the decade.

HONORING ROCK AND ROLL

The Rock and Roll Hall of Fame organization had existed since 1983, but it finally opened its permanent home in Cleveland, Ohio, in 1995. World-renowned architect I. M. Pei designed the new museum on the shores of Lake Erie. Two of rock's own architects—Chuck Berry and Jerry Lee Lewis—performed at the opening ceremonies, as did Bruce Springsteen, the Kinks, Johnny Cash, and the Pretenders. The museum houses both permanent and changing exhibits of rock memorabilia, from John Lennon's guitar to the Supremes' gowns to Michael Jackson's sequined glove.

ALTERNATIVE ROCK

Rock music has often been reactive. Genres frequently become popular because they are musical responses to other genres. Sometimes these responses are driven by economics, as certain segments of society do not see themselves reflected in popular music. Just as punk developed among the working class in response to corporate rock and the slick sounds of disco in the 1970s, an alternative form of rock, one that rejected the techno-sounds of new wave, achieved broad popularity in the early 1990s.

This stripped-down, angry rock had its roots in the alternative music scene. During the 1980s the Georgia-based band R.E.M. achieved cult status while recording for independent labels, laying the foundation for alt-rock's success in the 1990s. College radio stations were the first to embrace the music of R.E.M., Sonic Youth, The Pixies, and other alternative rock bands, as well as other burgeoning music forms.

GRUNGE

In the Seattle area, alt-rock was known as grunge. In some ways, a line can be traced from grunge back to the garage-band sound that Chuck Berry pioneered in the 1950s. Yet grunge was more aggressive in its musical approach, heavily dependent on wide variations in sound from quiet to noisy, in both its music and singing.

In 1991 Seattle's Nirvana released the album *Nevermind*, which included the single "Smells Like Teen Spirit." The song became an international hit and propelled the band's lead singer Kurt Cobain into reluctant superstardom. In 1994 he committed suicide, leaving behind a legacy as the spokesman for grunge.

A number of bands found a voice in alternative rock during the 1990s. Successful acts rising out of the alt-rock movement include the Smashing Pumpkins, Red Hot Chili Peppers, Jane's Addiction, Soundgarden, Weezer, and Pearl Jam, one of the decade's most popular rock acts who, like Nirvana, came from Seattle. Punk rock also entered the pop arena with the success of Green Day, a band from Berkeley, California. Pop-ska band No Doubt, fronted by Gwen Stefani, found success by blending Jamaican sounds with catchy melodies. Despite their origins in the alternative music scene, most of these bands went on to experience great commercial success.

BOY BANDS—INNOCENCE REGAINED

From the early days of rock and roll, vocal groups focused on harmony. In the 1950s and early 1960s, many of these groups sang in a rhythm and blues style known as doo-wop. Doo-wop grew out of African American urban communities in cities like

As lead singer of the Seattle grunge group Nirvana, Kurt Cobain became a superstar, but he arguably became more famous for his 1994 suicide.

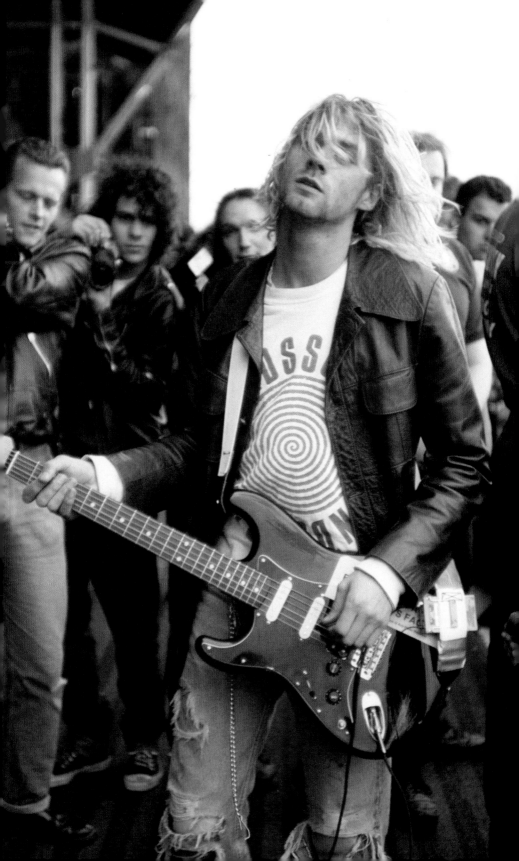

New York, Philadelphia, and Chicago, where young musicians often sang together on the streets. The style involves tight vocal harmonies. From the Drifters and the Platters in the 1950s to the Four Seasons and Gladys Knight and the Pips in the 1960s, doo-wop's strong harmonic influence prevails in popular music.

In the 1980s vocal groups consisting mostly of teenage and twenty-something boys began to attain wide commercial success: The broad popularity of two youthful groups, New Edition and New Kids on the Block, set the stage for the 1990s. In 1992, Motown's Boyz II Men—a quartet from Philadelphia—had an international hit with their song "End of the Road." All four members sang lead vocals, breaking the trend of a lead singer and a harmonizing backup. An English quintet called Take That experienced similar worldwide success with songs that topped the charts in Europe.

In the 1990s these groups became known as boy bands (though none of the members played instruments on stage). Instead the focus was on harmony and choreography, and the young men were often viewed as heartthrobs by adoring fans. The two most successful boy bands of the 1990s were 'N Sync and the Backstreet Boys—both of whom carried their enormous popularity into the next decade. In addition, 'N Sync launched the superstar career of member Justin Timberlake, who has become a successful solo artist, producer, and actor.

DIVAS RISING

Following Whitney Houston's stardom in the 1980s, a number of large-voiced women conquered the popular music charts in the 1990s. While the term *diva* traditionally applies to female opera singers, it became used frequently in the 1990s to describe female pop singers who had a strong stage presence to accompany their powerful voices. Two of the decade's most prominent divas were Mariah Carey and Celine Dion.

Mariah Carey and Whitney Houston are two large-voiced women who came to be affectionately called "divas" as their fame grew.

Singer and songwriter Mariah Carey is one of the most successful performers in the history of popular music, selling over 200 million records. Blessed with a stratospheric five-octave range (there are eight octaves on a piano), Carey's music has spanned dramatic ballads, catchy soul tunes, and hip-hop –inflected mid-tempo songs. Carey can be credited with bringing the singing style of melisma—applying more than one note to a syllable—to the forefront of popular music. Her influence has been far-reaching, as many young singers who have followed her have tried to achieve the same vocal acrobatics.

Canadian pop singer Celine Dion was born in Quebec and began her career singing in French. She had her first English language hit in 1990 with "Where Does My Heart Beat Now," but it was a duet of the title song for Disney's animated film *Beauty and the Beast* that propelled her into international fame in 1991. Her career was further solidified in 1997 by another movie song: "My Heart Will Go On" from *Titanic*. Both film songs won Grammy and Academy awards, and throughout the decade Dion experienced worldwide success for both English and French recordings.

MARY J. BLIGE

Rising out of the rap and hip-hop movements, singer-songwriter Mary J. Blige began her multi–platinum-selling career in 1992 with the release of her album *What's the 411?* With her large, expressive voice and dramatic gospel-tinged delivery, Blige merged hip-hop and soul. Throughout her career she has performed with an array of singers from other genres, including Elton John and opera singer Andrea Bocelli.

YOUTH MOVEMENT

In the late 1950s and early 1960s Disney's *The Mickey Mouse Club*, a children's television show, launched the singing and acting career of teenage star Annette Funicello. In the late 1990s several former members of a mid–'90s version of the Disney program found a wide audience. Justin Timberlake was a star on *The Mickey Mouse Club*, as was his 'N Sync band-mate J. C. Chasez. Starting with her 1999 mega-hit ". . . Baby One More Time," Britney Spears established herself as an international pop icon and one of the most successful women in commercial music. Another former star of *The Mickey Mouse Club* is the petite but huge-voiced Christina Aguilera—who also records in Spanish. She burst on the music scene in 1999 with her hit "Genie in a Bottle." Aguilera is renowned for her powerful, soulful voice and vocal acrobatics.

Also in the late 1990s, a young female quartet called Destiny's Child brought hip-hop to a mainstream audience, thanks in great part to their multitalented lead singer Beyoncé Knowles. The group soared to fame when it became a trio in the 2000s, launching Beyoncé's stellar solo career as a singer and an actress.

THE REAL SLIM SHADY

The world knows rapper Marshall Bruce Mathers III by his stage name, Eminem. After some work on independent labels in the mid–1990s, Eminem released his first major studio album, *The Slim Shady LP*, in 1999. Produced by respected rapper Dr. Dre, the album featured extremely violent and sexually explicit lyrics that straddled the line between dark comedy and psychosis. Still, it was an instant success, entering *Billboard*'s rap chart at number two and winning a Grammy award for Best Rap Album. More importantly, it launched Eminem's career as a musician and an actor—and as one of the most successful hip-hop artists.

SINGER-SONGWRITERS

Three women helped to redefine the singer-songwriter of the 1990s. Canadian singer Alanis Morissette created a sensation with the provocative lyrics in her album *Jagged Little Pill* (1995). Born in Homer, Alaska, Jewel crafted thoughtful folk songs recalling the singer-songwriters of the 1970s. Sheryl Crow blended elements of folk, rock, and blues into catchy tunes like "All I Want to Do" (1994). As a sign of the diminishing influence of folk on popular music, both Crow and Jewel have found more success in country music.

COMMERCIALIZED COUNTRY

Country music has a long history of crossing over into pop on the U.S. music charts. As pointed out earlier, some of rock's first stars were country artists like Elvis Presley and Bill Haley. In the 1960s country singers like Roger Miller, Johnny Cash, Glen Campbell, and Bobbie Gentry had hits on the pop charts. In the 1970s artists including the Eagles, Linda Ronstadt, and Jackson Browne crafted a hybrid of country and rock sounds.

And the music of country superstars Kenny Rogers and Dolly Parton had wide commercial appeal in the 1980s.

During the 1990s two country acts experienced unprecedented crossover success: Garth Brooks and Shania Twain. Garth Brooks began his career as a traditional country singer with songs like "Unanswered Prayers" and "Friends in Low Places" (both in 1990). Soon, he began to apply the wild theatrics of arena rock to his sold-out performances with results that were commercially spectacular. Brooks even outsold the Beatles in sheer numbers of records sold in the 1990s. His 1997 album *Sevens* debuted at number one on *Billboard* magazine's Top 200 Albums chart, a first for a country artist. Like Mariah Carey, as of 2011 Brooks has sold some 200 million records.

Singer-songwriter Shania Twain was born in Canada but made an indelible mark on the Nashville country music scene in the 1990s. In 1995 her second album, *The Woman in Me*, spawned a number of hits, including "Whose Bed Have Your Boots Been Under," "Any Man of Mine," and "(If You're Not in It for Love) I'm Outta Here!" The album eventually sold an unprecedented 18 million copies, making Twain the best-selling female country artist to date. In the 1990s Twain won Grammy awards in both country and pop categories.

MURDERING COUNTRY MUSIC?

While no one can deny the overwhelming success of Brooks's and Twain's music, many country purists were unhappy with the two singers' pop and stadium-oriented sounds. In 1999 two traditional country stars—George Strait and Alan Jackson—recorded "Murder on Music Row," a song lamenting country music's move into pop and rock sounds. It resonated so much that in 2000 the song appeared on *Billboard*'s country music charts even though it had never been released as a single!

FESTIVALS

For decades, festivals—from folk and bluegrass to jazz and pop—have been an important venue for music acts in many genres. The first successful rock festival was the Monterey International Pop Festival, held in 1967 in Monterey, California, featuring Jimi Hendrix, the Doors, and Janis Joplin.

In the 1990s, Lollapalooza and Lilith Fair, two hugely popular festivals, brought new sounds to music lovers and also served charitable and political purposes. Lollapalooza is an annual festival driven by the emerging acts in alternative rock. Perry Farrell, the lead singer of Jane's Addiction, created the festival in 1991. It features hip-hop, punk, and heavy-metal music. Acts have included Pearl Jam, Red Hot Chili Peppers, Rage Against the Machine, and Soundgarden. Lollapalooza is

Lollapalooza—a traveling festival—was a major venue for up-and-coming alternative rock bands throughout the 1990s and again in the early 2000s.

a traveling festival—not a one-time event like Woodstock. It ran until 1997 and was revived in 2003.

In 1997, singer-songwriter Sarah McLachlan founded Lilith Fair, a traveling festival featuring female artists and female-led bands. Lilith Fair ran until 1999 and—in addition to exposing women artists to a broader audience—helped to raise money for women's charities. Acts appearing in the festival included Tracy Chapman, Mary Chapin Carpenter, Jewel, and Emmylou Harris. Lilith Fair was revived in the summer of 2010.

ACCESSING MUSIC

Although many performers still refer to their releases as "records," recorded music has taken many forms in the last five decades. In the 1950s, although LP records (or albums) already existed, the arrival of the 45–rpm record—with one song on each side—helped enable individual songs to become hits. Music lovers bought a record for the hit song on the A-side, which they heard on the radio or on a jukebox, and got the B-side song as a bonus (although B-sides sometimes also became hits!).

In the 1970s records had to compete with various forms of tapes, from eight-tracks tapes to compact cassettes. These tapes allowed listeners to play music in their cars or on portable devices, further solidifying popular music's influence on culture.

Tapes often have a short shelf life, however, and in the 1980s the CD appeared. One of the main advantages of the CD—other than its small size—was the clarity of sound it produced. It could also hold much more music than a record. With the CD, music entered the digital age, and people began to replace their old albums with newly mastered CDs. The early twenty-first century would bring a major revolution in the way people accessed music, thanks to the Internet, MP3 players, and iTunes. Afterward, the music industry would never be the same.

THE 2000s:
Culture of Communication

IN JUNE 2002 TELEVISION VIEWERS ALL ACROSS the United States tuned in to a new reality program based on a televised singing contest called *Pop Idol* in England. *American Idol* would soon become one of the most successful shows in the history of television. To date, *American Idol* is the *only* television show to be number one among viewers for six consecutive years.

Idol has spawned the careers of a number of prominent pop stars, including first-season winner Kelly Clarkson and country superstar Carrie Underwood, the fourth-season winner. Even contestants who did not win the competition have made their mark. Third-season contestant Jennifer Hudson, for example, went on to win an Academy Award in 2007 for her role in the movie musical *Dreamgirls*, loosely based on the story of the Supremes.

The show's enormous success is indicative of the changing way that music reaches the public and influences popular culture. That a talent show in which young singers cover songs from the previous fifty years has become such a phenomenon illustrates how deeply popular music has permeated American culture.

Kelly Clarkson owes her musical career to a winning stint on the first season of *American Idol*.

DIMINISHING VENUES

Despite the undeniable success of *American Idol*, few variety shows remained on television by 2000. From the 1950s through the 1970s, acts as diverse as Elvis, the Mamas and the Papas, the Doors, and the Carpenters gained popularity by appearing on variety shows like *Ed Sullivan*, *The Carol Burnett Show*, or *The Hollywood Palace*. In the 1980s the weekly show *Solid Gold* offered a popular showcase for current and established music acts, and MTV and VH1 played music videos round-the-clock.

Few such venues existed for musical acts by the turn of the century. Bands might appear on late-night talk shows, morning news programs, Superbowl half-time shows, and the occasional televised special or awards show, but the country was no longer watching professional performers sing nightly on television. By 2000, even the music channels MTV and VH1 had stopped showing videos in favor of reality programs and nostalgic countdown shows.

The culturally unifying factors that made everyone from children to their grandparents aware of the same musical performers in the earlier days of popular music barely existed by 2000. Technology was moving music's focus away from being a cross-cultural event and into the personal realm.

DOWNLOADING TUNES

With the advent of the digital format, consumers in the first decade of the twenty-first century—often referred to as the "aughts"—discovered a new and powerful way to access music. Consumers could now download and share music files in MP3 format or purchase songs from the popular iTunes music store. Listeners could download individual songs and no longer needed to purchase entire albums. Instead, they could choose which songs they wanted to own and in some cases, which version of those songs they preferred. (Especially since the rise of hip-hop—but even long before that—music is often remixed into longer, danceable tracks for clubs.)

Pop music performers faced challenges in this new environment. First, music was often pirated—or accessed and downloaded—without being purchased. This was a serious copyright problem in the early days of the MP3, mainly because of a website called Napster that enabled the free sharing of MP3s. Second, the ability to purchase only the songs a listener wants took a huge slice out of the market for album sales. Finally, performers and record labels have had to find new ways to market their music to the public. Talent scouts have even begun to use the Internet as a tool to find new artists: videos posted on the popular website YouTube by aspiring musicians have spawned new careers.

The band Metallica went to war against Napster, charging that it illegally downloaded its music. Lars Ulrich, of the band, talked to reporters about the court battle, which the band won.

These changes, and the loss of album sales as the major source of popular music, created a crisis for the music industry. Producers looking to make profits in such a difficult market began to place greater emphasis on finding the next quick success. Therefore, popular music has become more disposable in recent years, resulting in less of a lasting cultural effect.

MERGING GENRES

In 2002 traditional country singer Johnny Cash covered the song "Hurt," written and recorded in 1994 by the industrial rock band Nine Inch Nails. This merging of artists, generations, and genres would have been unheard of forty years earlier. Cash was seventy-one years old when the video for "Hurt" was released. At the beginning of the video craze in the 1980s, no seventy-year-old artist would have received any airplay on MTV. However, Cash's video for "Hurt," directed by Mark Romanek, won a Grammy for Best Short Form Music Video, and is considered to be one of the most powerful and influential music videos ever made.

In 2004 country singer Loretta Lynn—at the age of sixty-nine—released the album *Van Lear Rose*, produced by twenty-eight-year-old musician Jack White. Whereas Lynn

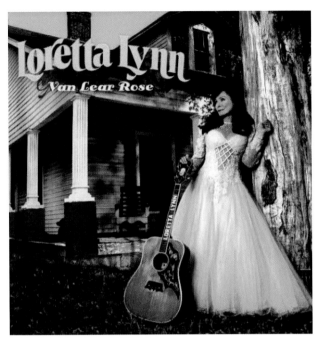

Who would've thought country music and punk rock could mix and end up a winner? *Van Lear Rose*, a collaboration between country singer Loretta Lynn and rocker Jack White, was just that. It won two Grammy Awards.

was famous as the coal-miner's daughter who sang traditional country songs about poverty, heartache, and infidelity, White came out of the rock tradition and had won critical acclaim with his first band, the White Stripes. He applied his rough-hewn garage-band sound to Lynn's compositions, and the album won two Grammy awards and great critical acclaim.

The success of *Van Lear Rose* points to the shifting way music is created and perceived in the twenty-first century. Many of the lines among musical genres have blurred and have thus created new genres.

EMO, AMBIENT, AND POP PUNK

Many of the new genres that came to the forefront of popular music in the first decade of the twenty-first century had formerly been peripheral genres, including emo, ambient, and pop punk.

Emo emerged from the hard-core punk scene of the 1980s and became part of the independent—or "indie"—music scene in the 1990s. It reached a more commercial audience in the early twenty-first century through bands like Dashboard Confessional and Taking Back Sunday. Emo is a more emotional form of punk, merging the intensity of the original movement with a romantic sensitivity in both its approach and lyrics.

Ambient music is characterized by its atmospheric sound, often mixing electronic and acoustic elements into textural sounds. The avant-garde composers John Cage and Brian Eno (who coined the term "ambient music") helped establish this genre in the 1980s. By the early twenty-first century, the British band Radiohead was blending elements of jazz and ambient music in their electronic sounds.

As the name implies, pop punk mixes elements of punk and pop music. Green Day has been the most successful group to come out of the genre, especially with their punk-rock opera *American Idiot* (2004). The album was so successful that it was eventually turned into a Broadway musical, running from 2010 to 2011. Rock's first opera had arrived in 1969 with *Tommy*—by the Who—about a physically challenged pinball wizard.

HIP-HOP, R&B, AND NEO-SOUL

Hip-hop (or rap) continued its dominance on the charts through the turn of the century. In many ways, hip-hop has become the pop music of the new millennium. Once considered part of the black urban scene, it has been embraced and performed by people of all backgrounds. Two of the decade's most successful hip-hop acts were Kanye West and the Black Eyed Peas. Others include 50 Cent, OutKast, Nelly, and Missy Elliott.

In the 1990s producers like Babyface, Jermaine Dupri, L. A. Reid, and P. Diddy, then known as Puff Daddy, began to merge elements of hip-hop with more traditional sounds from rhythm and blues (sometimes called R & B). At that time, huge commercial success came to acts like Ludacris, the female trio TLC, and accomplished showman Usher. In the following decade, a strong neo-soul movement developed, mixing sounds from hip-hop, rhythm and blues, jazz, and funk. A wide range of artists emerged from this movement, including Jill Scott, Alicia Keys, John Legend, and India Arie. These artists also blended elements of the singer-songwriter movement in their thoughtful lyrics, adding a new depth to hip-hop.

FROM BRITAIN WITH LOVE

At the turn of the century in Britain, a renewed interest in the Motown Sound (also known in Europe as Northern Soul) gave rise to retro-soul singers including Joss Stone, Estelle, Duffy, Adele, and the late Amy Winehouse. Their catchy melodies and soulful singing reveal strong influences from such 1960s singers as Gladys Knight, Aretha Franklin, and Dusty Springfield. In Britain, in 2011, Adele became the first artist since the Beatles to have two top-five hits in both the singles and album charts simultaneously.

GLEE

The enormously successful *Glee*, a television series about a high-school choral group, also known as a glee club, showcases pop hits of various genres and decades. On *Glee*, which first aired in 2009, the young cast frequently breaks into fantasy-like performances. Their songs range from forty-year-old pop standards and 1980s dance tunes to recent hip-hop songs and original music written for the show. The show has renewed interest in show choirs in high schools across the country. Like *American Idol*, on which contestants cover old Motown or classic rock songs, *Glee* offers another example of pop music's broad and lasting effect on popular culture.

HIGH SCHOOL MUSICAL

In 2006, the Disney Channel released the feature-length television movie *High School Musical*, about two high-school juniors—athletic Troy Bolton and nerdy Gabriella Montez—who try out for their high school's musical. Because they come from two different cliques, the first movie reminded many critics of Shakespeare's *Romeo and Juliet* (without the deaths). *High School Musical* was so successful that it spawned a sequel in 2007 and then a feature film in 2008. The soundtracks and DVDs of the films all became hits, especially among young teens.

YOUTH MOVEMENT

Pop music—especially since the advent of rock and roll—has had a long history of artists achieving success in their teens. In 1956 thirteen-year-old Frankie Lymon and his group, the Teenagers, produced one of rock and roll's first true classics: "Why Do Fools Fall In Love." Other teen acts have included Brenda Lee, Stevie Wonder, the Jackson 5, the Osmonds, Menudo, and Hanson. In the early twenty-first century, two more young performers became worldwide names: Taylor Swift and Justin Bieber.

At age sixteen, singer-songwriter Taylor Swift burst on the country-music scene in 2006 with her self-titled debut album and the single "Tim McGraw." The confessional nature of Swift's youthful lyrics struck a chord with audiences. She went on to sell millions of records and win numerous awards, including Album of the Year for her second album *Fearless* at the 2008 Grammy Awards and Entertainer of the Year from the Academy of Country Music in early 2011.

Justin Bieber was only thirteen years old when he was discovered, thanks to homemade videos his mother posted on YouTube. Bieber then got some important help from Usher, who signed the fledgling star to Island Records. Usher, along with prominent producers The Dream and Tricky Stewart, produced Bieber's first album, *My World*, turning him into an instant superstar when it was released in 2009.

The era of the Internet ushered in youth sensation Justin Bieber, who was discovered by way of YouTube.

LADY GAGA

She calls her fans "little monsters" and often wears outlandish outfits made of unusual materials, such as bubbles or meat. Despite her eccentricity—or perhaps because of it—Lady Gaga has become one of the most successful and influential singer-songwriters of the twenty-first century. Gaga's edgy stage presence owes much to performance art and the early glam-rock movement, as seen in the video of her hit "Poker Face" (2008). Her vocal style recalls singers like Madonna and Gwen Stefani, and her music reveals influences from the European techno-pop that became popular in the 1980s.

Lady Gaga has become a twenty-first-century phenomenon: a singer with a great voice and brilliant lyrics who has transformed her very persona into a performance piece.

Conclusion

FROM *AMERICAN BANDSTAND* TO *AMERICAN IDOL*, popular music has been in integral part of our culture. Once it achieved broad commercial appeal in the 1950s, popular music became both a reflection of the times and an influential cultural phenomenon. No one can deny the power of that music. People still recognize the music of the Beatles, the Supremes, Bob Dylan, Michael Jackson, ABBA, the Clash, and the Bee Gees. Time has not diminished its durability.

In recent years, genres that were once removed from each other have merged. Yes, pop music is ever-changing—but it is also part of a larger, ever-developing picture. Trends that seem original to a new generation of listeners often reflect those that have already come and gone.

Technology has become an increasingly influential factor in popular music. In 2010 the MTV Video Music Awards used Twitter to track the acts that were receiving the most attention from viewers and how quickly the conversation was moving among fans. Teenagers once held transistor radios in their hands just hoping to hear their favorite songs. Today, iPods and smart phones enable listeners to choose exactly which songs they want to hear—as well as when and how often. Who knows what the future holds for popular music?

Notes

CHAPTER ONE

p. 13, "Bob Dylan once said . . .": Stuart A. Kallen, *The History of Rock and Roll*, San Diego: Thomson Gale, 2003, 19.

p. 17, "Money to Burn": Statistics from Sarah Brash and Loretta Britten, eds., *Rock and Roll Generation: Teen Life in the 1950s*. Alexandria: Time-Life Books, 1998, 98.

p. 17, "Music of delinquents . . .": Kallen, *The History of Rock and Roll*, 23.

CHAPTER TWO

p. 25, "More than 73 million . . .": Stuart A. Kallen, *The History of Rock and Roll*, San Diego: Thomson Gale, 2003.

CHAPTER THREE

p. 35, "The record business . . .": Stuart A. Kallen, *The History of Rock and Roll*. San Diego: Thomson Gale, 2003, 72.

p. 38, "Over the next four decades . . .": Elton John News on Yahoo Music, www.new.music.yahoo.com/elton-john.

p. 40, "Pop music's most successful . . . ,": ABBA website, www.abba-site.com.

p. 44, "two-chord power pop . . .": Kallen, 91.

CHAPTER FOUR

p. 49, "melodic, catchy . . .": www.allmusic.com.

p. 50, "electronic effects . . .": Irwin Stambler, *The Encyclopedia of Pop, Rock and Soul*, rev. ed., New York: St. Martin's Press, 1989, 665.

p. 60, "a black cultural expression . . .": Stuart A. Kallen, *The History of Rock and Roll*. San Diego: Thomson Gale, 2003, 108.

p. 60, D.J. Kool Herc,: Kool Herc Biography, Old School Hip Hop website, www.oldschoolhiphop.com/artists/deejays/kooldjherc.htm.

CHAPTER FIVE

p. 65, "The museum houses . . .": Rock and Roll Hall of Fame Website, www.rockhall.com.

CHAPTER SIX

p. 80, "In the 1990s . . .": Anonymous, "Hip-Hop and Neo-Soul," Soul of America website, www.soulofamerica.com/atlanta-hip-hop-neo-soul.phtml.

p. 82, "Justin Bieber was only thirteen . . .": Justin Bieber Biography, Justin Bieber Official Website, www.justinbiebermusic.com/bio.aspx.

Further Information

BOOKS

Campbell, Michael. *Popular Music in America: And the Beat Goes On*, 3rd ed. New York: Schirmer, 2008.

Covach, John, and Dr. Mark Spicer. *Sounding Out Pop: Analytical Essays in Popular Music*. Ann Arbor, MI: University of Michigan Press, 2010.

Marks, Craig, and Rob Tannenbaum. *I Want My MTV: Story of the Music Video Revolution*. New York: Dutton, 2011.

Masar, Brenden. *The History of Punk Rock*. San Diego: Lucent Books, 2006.

Skancke, Jennifer. *The History of Indie Rock*. San Diego: Lucent Books, 2007.

Spitz, Bob. *The Beatles: The Biography*. Boston: Back Bay Books, 2006.

Taraborrelli, J. Randy. *Michael Jackson: The Magic, The Madness, The Whole Story, 1958–2009*. New York: Grand Central Publishing, 2010.

CDS

Gold Series. Hip-O Records. Series includes 2-disc sets on the 1960s, the 1970s, the 1980s, Classic Rock, British Invasion, Southern Rock, Soft Rock, Summer of Love (2005–2006).

DVD

The History of Rock and Roll. Time-Life Video. 2004. 5 discs. 578 min.

WEBSITES

Billboard Magazine
www.billboard.com
The website of *Billboard* magazine includes up-to-date music news and reviews. You can check the weekly charts, including the Hot 100, R&B/Hip-Hop, and Country, just to name a few. There's also a section on new releases, and you can look up information on various artists and listen to samples of their work.

The Grammy Awards
www.grammy.com
The official site of the Grammy Awards includes the history of the awards, downloads, news features, and media archives. You can read about the various nominees and watch videos of their performances on the Grammy Awards show.

Rock and Roll Hall of Fame
www.rockhall.com
The website of the Rock and Roll Hall of Fame includes videos and photos featuring inductees to the Rock and Roll Hall of Fame. Sections include the story of rock, the exhibitions, the inductees, education, and a shop.

Bibliography

The following is a selection of the material the author found helpful in his research.

Brash, Sarah, and Loretta Britten, eds. *Rock and Roll Generation: Teen Life in the 50s.* Alexandria, VA: Time-Life Books, 1998.

Dylan, Bob. *Chronicles: Volume One.* New York: Simon & Schuster, 2005.

George-Warren, Holly, Patricia Romanowski, and Jon Pareles, eds. *The Rolling Stone Encyclopedia of Rock and Roll.* New York: Fireside, 2001.

Kallen, Stuart A. *The History of Rock and Roll.* San Diego, CA: Thomson Gale, 2003.

Richards, Keith, and James Fox. *Life.* New York: Little, Brown and Company, 2010.

Stambler, Irwin. *The Encyclopedia of Pop, Rock and Soul,* rev. ed. New York: St. Martin's Press, 1989.

Index

Page numbers in **boldface** are photographs.

Murray, Anne, 39–40
music industry crisis,
 77–78
MTV (Music Television),
 46, 47–49, 56, 61, **61**,
 76–78, 85

Napster, 77, **78**
Nelly, 80
Nelson, Ricky, 20
neo-soul, 80–81
New Edition, 68
New Kids on the Block, 68
new wave, 49–51, 58, 65
Nicks, Stevie, 42, 58
Nine Inch Nails, 78
Nirvana, 66, **67**
No Doubt, 66
'N Sync, 68, 70
Nyro, Laura, 37

O'Jays, 41
Orbison, Roy, 12
Osmonds, 82
OutKast, 80

Parliament, 58
Pearl Jam, 66, 73
Peter, Paul and Mary, 28
Pink Floyd, 40, 41
piracy, 77
Platters, 68
the Police, 52
pop punk, 79, 80
popular music, 5, 6, 10
Presley, Elvis, 7, **8**, 12, 13, 71, 76
the Pretenders, 51, 65
Prince, 58
producers, 80, 83
progressive rock, 35
protest, 19, 28, **29**, 35, 54
psychedelic music, 26, 30, 32

punk rock, 44–45, **45**,
 49, 50–52, 65–66, 73,
 79–80, **79**

Queen, 40, 41
Queen Latifah, 61

race music, **8**, 10
Radiohead, 80
the Ramones, 44, **45**
rap, 60, 64, 70, 71, 80
Reddy, Helen, 40
regional sounds, 10, 41–42
R.E.M., 65
retro-soul, 81
rhythm and blues, 10–11, 13,
 17, 22, 26, 36, 55, 66, 80–81
Ritchie, Lionel, 56
Robinson, Smokey, and the
 Miracles, 11, **11**, 22
rockabilly, 12
rock and roll, 7, 26, 59
 birth of, 5, **5**, 7–17, 20
 business of, 35, 44
Rock and Roll Hall of Fame,
 65
Rolling Stones, 27, **27**, 28, 54
Ronstadt, Linda, 41, 59, 71
Ross, Diana, 23, 56
Run-D.M.C., 61, **61**
Rydell, Bobby, 20

Salt-N-Pepa, 61
Saturday Night Fever, 43, **43**
Sex Pistols, 45
Simon and Garfunkel, 28
singer-songwriters, 36–38, 50,
 70–72, 74, 81, 82
Slick, Grace, 30
 See also Jefferson Airplane
Sly and the Family Stone,
 32, 58

About the Author

MARK MUSSARI is a freelance writer, translator, and editor living in Tucson, Arizona. He received his Ph.D. in Scandinavian languages and literature from the University of Washington and taught for a number of years at Villanova University. He is the author of many nonfiction books including *Haruki Murakami* and *Amy Tan* in our Today's Writers and Their Works series. Dr. Mussari also served as the series consultant for the Pop Culture series.